My Own Name Seems Strange to Me

For Patrick,
With thanks and
all best wishes. Will
see you at AWP.
In frienship,
Tarn

My Own Name
Seems Strange to Me

poems by Karen Whalley

Off the Grid Press, Boston

Off the Grid Press is an imprint of Grid Books.

www.grid-books.org

Front cover: "Self Portrait," painting by Gabi Anderson, 2018.

Printed on acid-free paper by Thomson-Shore, Inc., Dexter, Michigan.
Book design by Michael Alpert.

ISBN: 978-1-946830-03-6

For Chris, Liz, Denny and Julia

Contents

My Own Name Seems Strange to Me

Naming It

Before dawn, from the gully where the creek abides
A bird whose name I do not know practices
Its five-note song, and I am a girl again
Sitting at the piano repeating a simple scale.

The bird sings, the sun rises, as if there were a connection,
And my feet do not reach the pedals as my hands
Spread, like wings, across the keys. The wound

Is easier to name: the father did not love,
And after that it was the husband, but the bird and the piano
Remind me of that man who read the same book
For thirty years, memorizing each sentence

As a way to perfect his understanding
Of the book whose name I never learned.
I would see him each morning on the corner
Waiting for the bus, the book spread

Across his hands, like wings at rest, peering into the pages
With his glasses slipping farther down his nose
So he had to tilt his head back as he stood there—

Dissolved into his book, like the bird dissolving
Into morning, the way the piano dissolves into the box of memory.

Snow Storm

All day, it fell:
The virginal world perched
Inside that white wing,
And the flaws disappeared
As in a fairy tale
Where innocence paints the landscape.

I thought I could hear it,
That soft falling, the accumulation
As it deepened outside my bedroom window.
The world was falling away
As the streets emptied,
Then filled again with laughter–
Even the parents sledded
The glistening grid of hills.

My life: I was warm;
I was drinking tea and reading
The thoughts of great men;
I was thinking back to an age
When the first love entered my life.
This great sadness
Began there, at that moment
Before which we can never return.

Somewhere, a phone was ringing
And the girl I was was listening
To her first lover,
Half-drunk and weeping with intoxication,
Saying the words, *I love you, dear.*

Even now, I believe him;
Even now, I know he was lying.
Maybe he wanted to mean it,

Like a robber who pockets a watch,
Stealing the life
Of someone who can afford watches.

Beautiful snow,

Fall on us all.
Make each life holy, again.
Let the thief into your deep robes.
Let the liar come clean.

Yoga Class

Sometimes, when I'm in *Downward Dog* or *Dancer,*
Which my doctor says will strengthen my bones,
I wonder if I am simply a product of a generation of narcissists
For which Americans are so well-known. When I look up

I can see the biceps of the football jock bending into his muscular version
of *Forward Fold,* and on the mat next to him, a woman
In leopard tights and a ponytail chewing her gum
And the older man with a knee replacement just doing

The best he can. For every flexing body in this room
There is a different reason and purpose: We aren't lilies
Of the field, neither spinning nor toiling, in our imperfect attempts
To exalt these bodies. We are not drinking from the fountain of youth

For God's sake, only inching toward death in a most graceful way.
Or, as the teacher says, *Connecting with ourselves,*
As if the self were another person (weak back, bad hip)
We were handed, like a foster child, to tend and feed

Before sending them out to be destroyed by the world.

Honey

During a bee's lifetime, she will make
approximately one teaspoon of honey.

At first, I see them as pathetic, flying around the yard,
Bumping into things, like bushes and windows and towels

Drying on the line. Are they blind, or confused,
Trying to figure out how to get from here to there

Without smashing into something huge, like the side
Of a house, or do they know what they are doing

Siphoning the nectar from the ragged dresses of peonies
And lilies? Then, I think they are heroic: a lifetime gathering

One teaspoon of honey, which is as much as most of us
Ever achieve. Think of all the traveling this entails,

All the hours spent searching for one drop of pleasure,
All the disappointment when you find a place discovered days ago

By someone else. But this is the way it is when you're an explorer:
You want to be the first to plant your flag and rape the fields.

But now I understand they are as ordinary as us, stuck in a world
Of dependencies and beauty: floating down into the open mouths

Of flowers, then rising up from the throats from which they carry
Sweet fluids, as if the flowers had just given birth.

Bella Rosa

I am listening to a conversation between two young women
Over toasted-marshmallow coconut lattes at Bella Rosa
Texting from their iPhones the friends who could not be here

When one of them says, "*Life is a comedy,*" to which the other agrees.
I stay buried in my book where Mary is watching her son
Drag his bloody cross up the hill, Mary thinking he's delusional

But he is her son, and she loves him, the two young women
Luminous with youth and the latest version of English
Creating a kind of joyous atmosphere in the coffee shop:

"*Then I said: Dude!*" and he said, "*Shut up!*" which means
Unbelievable. Being middle-aged, I have permission to listen,
And to read alone at a table;

At this age, I can be surrounded by the silly commotion
Of sexy, clinging tops and the Italian boots of the baristas
And know that life is tragic: that long red nails

And a bracelet of flowers tattooed around an ankle are just a chapter
Before the real story begins, before we say, "*Once, I was...*"
When all the dying selves we were become the funeral it is.

About Cats

About cats, I know nothing, but this one rubs against my leg
Asking in her wordless way to be my friend. Without language,
I am left with interpretation; without interpretation I am lost.

But how do you turn away a thing that must need a mother?
This much, I know: Love is a requirement, and the cat comes
Inside without an invitation and finds the rocking chair

A suitable place to sleep. I never much liked cats:
Their shredding claws, their allergic drifting hair
And indifference, that superior air of people living in the city.

She is lucky I miss my son, whose body curled against my own,
A small replica of us, as we read his childhood books, who banged
On the table before his dinner was served, like a tyrant or a king.

And don't I know how to please anything demanding? Oh, I do.
I dice the leftover chicken into tiny bites and set it in a dish
On the kitchen floor, where she sniffs, as if she were indignant,

As if she were my prisoner, now that I have let her in.

A Face at the Window

My friend's young son howls when he sees the moon,
Not yet knowing the word *m-o-o-n*, just the primal plaintive cry
Of longing all animals make on a cold night outdoors.

He lifts his little face, purses his lips into a kiss
And releases his pitiful cry, as if the moon were his mother
So far away he wants her back. He stands in his crib

Scanning the sky for the bright torch of her face:
A lonely baby calling his constant, touching the window
Where his own face floats just below the moon's.

Selling the Old Family Volvo

The young couple and their two small sons
Drive from the city to pay for and take the keys

To my old family Volvo—a car, like a house,
Full of memories, full of departures and returns.

They swarm inside as if it were a hive,
The children bouncing on the seats, the mother admonishing,

Though I anticipated sadness, their joy overcomes me,
The joy of something new and unfamiliar, the history

That will begin with their journey back to where they live.
The last vestige of our marriage: I imagined I would cry

As the husband pulls away from the curb and the wife
Follows in the car they had driven so far to get here

With their cargo of kids and a cooler full of food.
But I smile and wave from the front steps in early summer

As they drive away, amazed at their good luck.

Vernacular

I love that phrase, *Back in the day,*
Because it means you have a memory,
That, once, things were somehow better,
That country from which you immigrated to build
A different life. Or, maybe, you lived through a war,
The personal kind, where your parents were your enemy,
Where your ex-husband or ex-wife found what they mistook for love
In a chat-room on the internet.

Sometimes, I drive by the house in which we lived:
The white gate swung open, the house rising out of its meadow,
And everything I used to be is like someone I divorced
Against my will. Someone died, and it was me.
I want to say I loved that woman, her fidelity to a cold man
Her lack of anger at the pain.

Who is this now who could destroy the teenager
Whose awful music vibrates from his car, invading
The thought she's trying to think at the moment
Traffic stalls to let an elk cross the highway to the safety
Of the other side. Once, I would have understood
That part of youth is to be a huge imposition on the world,
But now that time is running out,
I want the kid behind the steering wheel
To turn the volume down and watch the grace
With which the elk dignifies that space between the cars.

Testament

I was in a practical mood, pulling out the flowers,
Chopping the stalks where the garden had exploded
In a manic state of propagation. Then it seems
I wept a little, as if my father's death were somehow part
Of my decision to austere my yard. And now I see
Hollyhocks protruding from the dirt,
Framing the doorway with their purple fans, claiming their right
To resurrect, which the Jehovah's Witnesses coming down the block
Would say is the metaphor for Christ.

All the things I dreamed would happen never happened;
All the things I dreaded became defining chapters of my life,
But I don't cut down the crops, nor spray them with the poison
It would take to kill a thing that's only proving itself.
Beauty won't be extinguished by the likes of me:
A woman in a floppy hat and work gloves, the sun
Depositing its little cancers in my skin, the sun extracting
Flowers from the ground—a flock of perching birds.

Places We Die

Patricia, for instance, sat at her desk every day
Hunched over the numbers an auditor requires,
Because there are people who spend their lives counting,
And the order of that must feel like safety or finding truth
In math. Hers was not a life of a mystic or philosopher:
The day began, the day ended, and in between the stacks
Of paper mysteriously diminished, like a glacier
Whose measurements no scientists can agree on.

Every noon, to the minute, she walked to the city pier
Where her husband waited in their little boat,
And he rowed her around the harbor as she ate the lunch
He had prepared: always tuna fish with the crusts
Trimmed carefully from the bread—that was his song and his gondola.
Forty years a plain woman is adored by a kind man,
Both punctual, both with a proclivity to repetition,
And behind the outward boredom, a romance flourished
As only in the secret rooms of history.

It was a Monday, and all we saw was Patricia rising from her chair,
Patricia falling, Patricia on a stretcher covered with a sheet,
The medics not even trying anymore. That's how simple
It is, when one moment you are adding up some information
And the next you are stepping into death, and who can win
Against a truck built that big?

And maybe it makes you want to go home and make love
To your husband, or chew your food more slowly;
Maybe you pick up an ordinary leaf and say, like a penitent,
All that was familiar is foreign to me, now.

A Public Moment

If only I could remember the name of the book,
But I remember the word: *canary*, a small, largely yellow bird
Of the genus *Dendroica*. In first grade, a word on a page
Is not yet a sound, so I looked at the word and thought *cannery*,
And asked to read that word, I read it wrong.

The class laughed.

The class laughed and then grew silent in the seriousness of my mistake,
But Mrs. Ross asked what else that word might be.
Someone gives us a second chance, and that becomes the hole
In the fabric of a self through which our infant indignation rises.
So I said it again, *can-a-ry*, and everyone applauded.

This is for you, Donald McKenzie, who sang *McNamara's Band*
Before the class in your silly kilt on St. Patrick's Day,
And for you, Steve Champion, with your awful runny nose,
And also, Marcia Waldron, you with your needle and diabetic lunches,
Who may not know how I swore I would never be laughed at again.

I ought to thank you.

Now, when someone laughs, I hear the cruelty behind the intention
Of the laugher, and I watch the anger arc steadily as a sunrise
In the face of the laugh's object. Maybe I learned, all those years ago,
Not to trust the happy and not to fear the sadness of a human face
Where the riots of injustice are burning the cities of the strong.

Appearances

In all the old photographs, my sister, brother and I
Solemnly stand with our sad small faces, my sister and I in our
Little white gloves and patent leather Mary Janes, my brother
In his red crew cut, fresh from a spanking. It is not only in the pictures

That we look frozen—we are frozen in our life, waiting for
The next uproar in which He Who is Short of Temper
and She Who is Hysterical will break an Irish Waterford lamp
Or pitch the polished sliver onto the manicured grass,
As if a picnic had just taken place.

This morning, I left the dishes in the sink, and October leaves
Are an explosion on the lawn, and I am writing in my pajamas,
Because I don't want the burden of anyone thinking I am perfect.
I don't want to romanticize the past, even as I know

Remembering is its own kind of punishment. The sky's a gorgeous blue
Today, calm and deep as a Cape Cod pond, but the weatherman on NPR
    predicts
A war of thunder later this evening. My neighbors' basement flooded.
That blue heaven isn't steady; it's just propped up.

As If

When my mother pointed the pistol
At my father in the middle of the living room
In the middle of the night
I stood in my white nightie
At the end of the tunnel
Of the long dark hall
And thought my life was ending,
Meaning we three children
Would be forever shuffled
From home to home, handed over
Like free kittens in a cardboard box
To strange people with hearts.

That is how I learned the art of detachment
How again and again death circled without landing,
How I could watch, imagining every possible outcome:
The red spinning wail of an ambulance
Parked at our front door,
The sheeted stretcher bearing him away from us,
The dark forest that would fall, from which we'd never emerge.
But not yet, that small scream
Rose and died on the smallest wave of hope inside my chest.
Then the make-up kiss when my father
Talked the gun onto the table,
And I'd watch him leave for work
The next morning with his lunch
And his thermos, and how did he live a split life like that?

Even now, I think someone should arrest my mother:
We were orphans with parents,
Though at dinner we sat like a family
And in the long pew at church.
When the minister spoke of the woman
Who was stoned, when Christ hung from the cross
In the sanctuary.

Paradise

At the trailhead, a sign reads: *Caution: Bears*
And you pause for a moment trying to decide if you
Want to take the only life you have into the hills

Where the rules of human conduct do not apply, and you
Are food. But you push yourself along the shaded path
Heading into deep territory a little nervous and singing

So the bears will hear you coming—a ranger suggested this—
And armed with only the words to *The Tennessee Waltz*
You leave the parking lot behind, as if it were your mother,

And who would know if you got into a wrestling match
With a bear whose cubs were not far off shaking huckleberries
From a bush or drinking from a mossy-bottomed stream

And how would you explain your way out of this since you
Don't even speak the same language as the claws
And the fangs sink into your leg—no questions asked.

So you begin to regret your choices and negotiations
Have seriously broken down as the woods grow darker
While back in town the population hovers at 17,000

And at least you know the names of those you shouldn't trust.

Dental Clinic

Across the yard   beyond the fence
The lights of the dental clinic   shine on dark mornings
And I can see the patients   lying back in their leather recliners
Their little paper bibs   tucked above their shirts

With the dentist looking down   into their mouths
And the patients looking up   at the long fluorescent lights.
Trust fills the room   like the scent of antiseptic
And the caretaker   and the cared for are one

As in a marriage.   He promises to be careful
She promises to hold still   or turn her head *that way*
To accommodate his reach.   The grinding, whining drill
Molds the bowl   into which the filling pours.

Now sit up   and let me wipe the corners of your mouth.

Conversation Among Geese

All morning geese have been rowing above my backyard
Making the noise geese make: not a honk exactly, or a cry
Just broken syllables, like the stutter of breathless runners.

The yards are empty of flowers, but the house across the street
Dazzles with Christmas lights, Mary and Joseph standing
In their ancient robed poses, with Santa on one side

Reindeer on the other, a scene as dissonant as Bethlehem
And Walmart, as odd as hope and commerce. I know my neighbor
Wants his daughter to be happy, and she claps her hands

As he plugs in the lights at the sight of the small Las Vegas
Of their yard, though Mary never says a word, just looks
Down at the infant. I want to believe in the star and the manger,

Without the crucifixion, but I admire the geese for knowing
When to leave, their wings pumping in white waves
Bearing them farther and farther toward some imagined home.

Donation

The girl ringing the Salvation Army bell outside Safeway,
Whose enviable kind face stares at the rows of cars
In the parking lot, not looking at the people who do not give—
She's that polite. As if I were giving to her personally,
I take from my wallet one ten-dollar bill and drop it into the kettle

Because I want her to be successful at her job; I want her to like me.
I am not a good person; I am only trying to make the world
A little more fair, level the playing field,
Tilt luck in someone's direction. And the man playing violin
In the rain, his case open for a few dull coins, his sweatered dog lying,

Like slippers, at his feet, should I also give to him?
The master and his servant. And should I also be giving
To the kid who needs a new kidney, cans with his picture taped on them
On counters all over town? Saving myself
Has been a grueling piece of work, and sometimes I just need

To watch the seasons change colors and shapes,
Scents and flowers; I just need to watch the grey winter birds
Find what they are looking for in the ragged, god-forsaken shrubs;
I just need the grass to stay grass-like
Not asking for my approval or allegiance or love.

In Green Pastures

The bars and gyms and grocery stores
Are full of lonely people, filling their carts and baskets
With lotions and frozen dinners, or watching television
Where a channel is an eye into a world. Maybe the problem
Is that I don't have a favorite team for which to root.
But there is always some kind of ball involved
And I want my loyalty in person, like the mailman
Wearing shorts in winter, whose love of uniforms
Began as a cub scout, whose love of country
Began with the first grade pledge of allegiance,
Who knows the routine of nine o'clock rounds.

Oh, that flag was new and beautiful flapping in the wind
Above Monroe Elementary, where Mrs. Ross
Told us where to hang our coats. Still, I need
To get a television so I can sit in my recliner,
Which I would have to buy, and watch the evening news.
If you don't own a television, you may as well
Live in a third world country, you may as well
Walk down to the river and beat your jeans and towels
Against a rock to get them clean, because all
This loneliness is a product of not taking the time
To lie down in some green pasture while the man
You love is removing all your clothes.

In the Backyards of Summer

Two doors down, the grandmother is watering her parched plants,
The girl riding her trike back and forth across the patio's grey desert
When she stops and notices the dying flowers in their beds
And asks, *"What happened to the flowers?"* From where I hear them

Beyond the hedge, I can only imagine the limp and drooping heads
That stood at attention early summer, crisp in their bright uniforms.
But a child has asked a question that deserves an explanation,
So the old woman heaves herself up from her knees and answers,

"They have lived their lives." It was a beautiful question asked
In the sweet, high voice of a child, and it was a beautiful answer
In the tired, wise voice of age, and somewhere between innocence
And the inevitable giving in to time, I find myself smiling as I examine

The closed purses of what will be a shock of blue clematis
Climbing an explosion of roses. I remember telling a student once,
"People don't fail, they just quit," when he thought language
And interpretation were beyond him, but he stayed and he studied

And he asked, *"What is a sentence?"* and looked at me and waited.
He needed an answer, so I opened a book and lifted up a piece of chalk.

Knowing Both

When her sister was lying in a hospital bed
With one breast and just flat stitched skin
Where the other had been, wondering
How something you love can kill you, my friend picked up
A book lying on the stainless steel table,
Which happened to be a book of poems my other friend
Had written, I saw how connected we are, as if the pain
Of his poems were an ointment to the soul
That tends the spirit of the flesh.

I love my poet friend for writing that book,
Pouring it all out like a fine wine from the vessel
Of himself, and I love the friend whose sister
Loved that book, sipping from it, then putting it down
Then raising herself up to sip from it again.

From my study window, I look out on the desolation
Of winter, all the damage of wind and rain and sleet,
And though we call the garden *dead*, we also know
That it is necessary to die a little each day
In order to be born again as something else.

My friend's sister was lying on the beach of that ocean
Of poetry, listening to its waves, and my other friend
Didn't know he had thrown her a little boat,
That the boat he had built to save himself
Was also saving her, and I knew someone she had known,
And he had reached out from his cabin thousands of miles
Away and told her exactly what she needed to hear
With his sad and gorgeous songs.

Movie

For just ten dollars, you can buy a few hours
In a cool, dark room, you can sip soda through a plastic straw,
Dip the tips of your fingers into a buttery bucket of corn
And watch the lives of other people, as if observing
From your chair the laboratory of your species.
And you can identify with the beautiful heroine,
And you can curse the woman who hates
The goodness of her sister, you can hope the mean-spirited kid
Who taunts the one in glasses dies—you don't have to do anything
But rest like a spider in its silken hammock
Swaying in the breeze. You can enter and love the subject of the story,
Which is the victory of the underdog, the nerdy philosophical orphan
Whose lack of cool refreshes you, like a childhood lake.

Murdering the Bird

Here I am in paradise: sunny outside, breeze enough
To waltz the bushes back and forth, the songs
Of yard birds a music you can't dance to, but they sing

Anyway, the one melody they are given. The neighbor's cat
Is lounging in the shade eyeing a particularly handsome
Red-chested fellow I can't find in my *Book of Birds*

And the cat springs taut as an arrow from its bow
And knocks the bird from a low-hanging branch
In a pusillanimous act of aggression, and before

I can stop her, the injured flight of the bird
Takes it to the nearest tree, screeching with disbelief,
Trembling before it drops like a fallen star to oceanic grass.

"Does one bird matter to the world?" I ask myself
Refusing to be horrified once more by death's
Bloody statistics, refusing to mourn again the fact

That death wants to make a prisoner of beauty
And beauty can't fly fast enough to outrace, if not this cat,
Then another, and for some reason I remember

My father saying of a judge who had molested a child,
My father, who lived beyond all knowledge, *"Probably,
That little girl wanted it,"* as if to blame the prey.

News

In her letter, my friend sends me a picture
Of the hurricane sweeping her street with water
Whipped into meringue by beating winds. The cost
Of a house on the Atlantic is the damage
Of a voyage through cruel elements, but Anne
Bakes bread to take to the neighbors, while the phone lines
Snap and vibrate, like the strings of a violin
Played by an inebriated god. Mashing bananas
By candlelight, I'll bet she is humming, setting out
More candles in every trembling room.

Here, in the calm of a crimson October,
I set the grinning pumpkin on my porch,
Wondering how many autumns I get to witness
The leaves falling, like money, lucky for the privilege
Of this ordinary existence. Last week, the doctor said
Some cells were fighting a war somewhere inside me
And I imagined my death and I imagined my life forever changed,
But Anne would bake a pie right now, because you have to love
The things you know you're going to lose,
Because the aftermath of catastrophe is this strangely descending joy.

Rain

As if they were giving birth,
The clouds opened to let the waters out,
And though I know the theory
Of condensation and atmospheric pressure,
I can almost believe, for a moment,
A benevolent god is showing mercy
On the parched desert of the lawn.

Only because I am middle-aged,
Only because my life so far
Resembles a really bad movie
With a twisted plot of characters
Who are neither interesting nor loyal,
Can something like rain
Relieve me of the burden of those memories.

Sometimes, in the morning,
Before the cars parade toward work,
I see an old woman, or an old man,
Walking a dog along the sidewalk.
And my heart breaks
Like a shattered dish
Because I love them, the quiet people
Who no longer explain the life behind them:
Old man, old woman who didn't quit

The corroded engines of their hearts
Chugging them past the docks
With the boats moored in consecutive order,
Like a sentence, rocking in those gentle waters.

Once, I prayed to die but didn't,
So I painted my bedroom a soft shade of green.

Saying No

Dating seems like fishing: some you just have to throw
Back into the river; sometimes you are lesson thirty-two
On their slow path to recovery, and sometimes you
Are simply an experience

Like a ferris wheel ride at the county fair,
But a man I dated three years ago
Wants another chance—he's polished his slow pitch,
He's practiced his apologies in front of a mirror

But repeating the past is like reading the same sad novel
Over and over, and now that I've had therapy, I know
That the disappointment I would feel is the same disappointment
I felt for my father—may his ashes rest in White Creek.

So I say *no*, and no one's heart is broken,
No one walks away crying into a handkerchief or tissue,
No one's wasted time or paid a check at a restaurant
For an expensive dinner for two.

This morning, rain pecked at my bedroom window
Like the beaks of a thousand tiny birds, and I woke to no one's arms;
The neighbor's Christmas lights were off so that the tree
In his window was exactly like the tree growing in his yard;

I want to be that splendidly unadorned, which is to say
I want to be that honest.

Son

When the weatherman on the radio announces,
"A one hundred percent chance of rain today,"
The certainty of what will not happen in the form
Of a lawnmower or pruners shapes this morning.

How could I have known that the white dress I wore
Down the aisle on my father's arm would be the last thing
I packed, moving in the aftermath of that particular forever?
I don't make promises, anymore, that I might break.

But I promised you a birthday party, candles
Extinguishing in your one big blow and the clapping
Of your many friends, followed by the disappointment
Of torn paper and bows scattered, as if a storm had traveled through.

I, who want nothing to ever end, oh, I grieve each dumb rose
Fallen, like a soldier, in the war of beauty in the world,
Just as I will grieve this whole damn day of rain
And the bright dot of carrot soup hardened on the stove

As if this home were a hotel, this world an airport of departures.

Spared

I had read that butterflies are becoming extinct,
And remembered, as a child, how I loved the white ones
And I probably held some superstitions back then

About how it fixed like a tattoo on the sleeve of my blouse—
Probably some idea I had about purity and God.
But this morning, as I was mowing the sloped front yard

A black one with identical buds of orange on each wing
In perfect symmetry fell in the path of the mower, and I stopped
Mid-yard, hoping it would helicopter straight up into air

But it struggled, its entire body vibrating in the wind
Of the whirring blades. It wasn't a bird I could nurse back to health
In a cardboard box, just a jewel in the satin grass

And I thought how when you can't save a living thing
You can go around it, or leave it alone, or let it find its own way
Of going on and getting well. Every day, something dies

Something beautiful vanishes or someone cuts your roses
When you aren't home and all you have is memory,
Memory like the powder on your fingers when, years ago,

You touched their wings, after which it was impossible for them to fly.

Woman at Car Wash

In summer, when the berries redden on the bushes
And the bedroom fan blows against the heat with the futility
Of a struck match in the aromatic dark, the cars
Line up at the car wash, veiled in dirt and insects

Glued to the windshields as the woman attendant
Takes your money, slaps a soapy rag across your hood,
A job like a factory worker or the "illegal immigrants"
Who pick clean row after row in the parched fields of July.

So I wonder as I wait to be pulled by the front tires
Into the belly of tunnel and brushes how she
Remains so cheerful day after day in the tourist sun,
Seeming to be happy even among the steaming buckets

Of water turning black with hubcap tar, her hair pulled
Back, her pants rolled up. Shouldn't I unlatch my seatbelt,
Climb out and grab a sponge to pull my weight? Or is it,
After all, my job to sit behind the steering wheel

Entering and exiting this tube of steam and suds and privilege
As she wipes her brown forehead with her dirty sleeve.

Wading Into the Lake

Across the street from my apartment
A fire truck and an ambulance, and there must
Have been a cop car, its red lights breaking
Up the dawn, night and morning changing shifts
Like the waitresses at the all-night diner.

I stood at the window as they chopped the ice,
And as it broke, they waded in and pulled from vast darkness
The body of an already stiff woman, long hair heavy
With lake water, and lying in a thin nightgown
That clung to her breasts, her thighs, her arms
White and lacy, like a bride.

I needed a story about why this woman
Would drive to the edge of a lake in the middle of night
In the middle of winter, what desperate thoughts
Had wakened her in the hours before or after,
And a man entered the story I was telling myself—I imagined
Him handsome—even as she lay
Spread across the grass, young still and beautiful,
The firemen and the cops just standing there
Talking and smoking in the cold.

New Day

At the New Day Cafe, an old guy in jeans and a t-shirt
Strums his guitar and sings in a voice that is a mix of Bob Dylan
And Arlo Guthrie songs he wrote praising his dead wife

As if the arguments and infidelities of forty years
Never happened and he's left to mourn the saint,
Which is harder than mourning the human who ate cold spaghetti

For breakfast or always squeezed the toothpaste from the middle
Of the tube. As the diners push away their plates or wipe a tear
They wonder if anyone will write a song about them when they die

The way, at my father's funeral, strangers stood up and told stories
About a man I couldn't recognize, a man I could have loved
If all those testimonies were true. But forgetting makes it possible

To live with the past or to think you had the life you always wanted
When really all you can do is go get some ice cream
And sit on a bench in the park where for once

What you want and what you get come together, before it starts to melt.

Hunters and Gatherers

What I know about our ancient ancestors is this:
The men hunted, the women gathered and gave birth
Beneath golden stalks of wheat and corn,

And this morning in the frozen winter yard beneath the cherry tree,
I saw them: pellets left by a wild animal that must have wandered
And stopped in my yard as I was sleeping,

And it's difficult to believe that in the modern world of cars
And television dishes and plastic green recycle bins
The primitive can still pierce our denial of our fear of beasts.

Remember that story of the child raised by wolves
And how he believed so fully in his wolf-ness that he howled like one?
And the one about the monkey raised by humans who ate his banana

With a knife and a fork, which makes me think biology concedes
To parenting, except that does not explain the elephant
Who still contained the rainforest deep inside him, enough to crush

His trainer into the sawdust of a circus in Miami. Whatever passed
Through my city lot, the sentinel inside me did not hear it
And maybe it was lost, trying to find the forest where it could safely hide

Among the leaves and the underbrush from the hunter with his spear,
Though no one hunts anymore, no one carries a bow and arrow
Just as I do not live inside the circle of a campfire with my tribe

But in the civilized world where the dangers are tame:
The sniper poised on a rooftop, the rapist hiding in the bushes,
The office flirt leaning close enough to smell his breath.

Bachelor

No tree, no red-ribboned gifts, no lights strung around a bush
Outside,

And in the corner of the kitchen, his cat is sleeping near the warmth
Of the stove,

While on the television a football game where the excited cries
Of a commentator is all the emotion he needs.

Recently, I read about the monks in Austria who pray all day
Just brewing beer to replace the abbey roof,

And of the starving children in *National Geographic* batting flies
From their bowls of rice.

If the monks choose a life of deprivation, as if it were an act
Of holiness,

The children dream of meat and milk and peace among
The naked, fighting tribes.

Oh, world, I love you—but. You are horrible and beautiful; you
Are peopled with the broken-hearted; the light of your many winters

Is weak; your roses melt as quickly as they are picked.
The bachelor places a candle on the table

Opens his book and begins his meager dinner, as the quarterback dances
And the flame leaps up the wick.

Little

My mother's favorite bird was the hummingbird,
Perhaps because she considered herself to be petite
And liked diminutive things, kept two chihuahuas
That slept in a basket near her own little bed.

She would hang a feeder from a low branch of a tree, a breast
Of red sugar water, from which they would drink, hovering
As if suspended from a thread, and sometimes lunging at each other
With their slender needle beaks. I can't see a hummingbird

Now helicoptering into my honeysuckle, the amazing machinery
Of their wings, without thinking of my mother, her fierce will
Clothed in flowered, ruffled prints, holding out a little finger
As she sipped her tea. I want to tell you something:

There are mothers who eat their young; mothers who drive
Their children into lakes. You will know them, the little mothers among us.

Red Religion

November, and every hillside
Is blazing, burning but not consumed
Like the bush of Moses
Hiding his face from his Lord.
Apples, like a sacrament,
Lie holy on the frozen ground;
The leaves, too, lie singed with this season:
Season of red, season of my chest
Aching with loss,
The overlay of childhood on everything.

Somewhere, my mother
Exists at many ages:
Braiding my hair, because she is angry
At my father and excludes him
From the rituals of her children,
Or grown old in her bathrobe
Where she has gone to die:
One room, one chair, in which
A thousand memories reside.

My father, too, is somewhere:
Young and full of good luck,
Money and charm, lifting the hands
Of women to his lips and placing a kiss
There, or old enough to have forgotten
The road, *this* road, that curves to his house:
Road of maples with its wooden bridge.
Whose house is that?

How many cold Novembers
In a life, but also, how few,
How each one stuns, as if it were the first,
And as if it were the last.

How cherished and indispensable
A month, how insufficient
The scarlet beads of rosehips
Flaring along the bent November twigs
I love like red religion.

Hansi says, *I will never be in the world*
In the same way.
Richard says, *It was almost a relief*
When he died.
World without them in it,
World that burns but does not burn up.

The Work He Does for Love

My neighbor might have broken up
With her boyfriend, who landscaped
Her yard, building little walls of brick
And paths of rock that curved like a picture
In *Sunset* around the corners of her house.
And he had planted flowers there, too,
Of varying size and color—
Lavender and roses, low lying forget-me-nots,
A plant with a name he probably hoped
Would represent his place inside her heart.

I used to watch him after work
Hauling wheelbarrows mounded with dirt
Back and forth, a large man driven to please her.
And afterward they'd sit on the steps
Holding a salute as the sun went down
Behind the mountains, like any couple
Sitting in the dusk.

But I don't see his black truck
Parked in front, anymore, and I don't see
His broad hand lifting from the rake
To wave as I leave for the store,
Or as I come home. The yard looks beautiful
Now, and the flowers are filling
Where the spaces were—I can feel myself
Wishing they had made it work,
Partly because I miss the *sweep, sweep*
Of his broom brushing cut grass
From the sidewalk, trying to earn
What should just be given. *Hey,*
I had called to him, balancing a bag
Of groceries on my hip, *The yard looks great.*

All Morning Long

Long morning, the shower raining down my back,
The coffee trickling into its pot, and me
Dividing my things into what I'd been given,
What I'd bought, and what my father had left
In the wake of his dying, and I thought,
It is time for a garage sale. I thought,
Too much stuff in a small house
Is a sign of spiritual deficiencies.

And the morning got longer the more I thought
About the list of things to do:
The wheat field my yard had become,
The liquid soap missing from the bathroom sink,
And the crows clamoring from the telephone lines
With their fuss and their gossip. Isn't it a sad world
When the mailman walks right by your box,
Little white oven on a red post, in his gray walking shorts
Bearing news and love letters and the bill
For your new white crown. A friend asked,
Is a bad day better than no day? She needs to ask
A philosopher. She needs to ask a priest.

Coffee

First thing in the morning
My father woke and rose
From the bed in which my mother
Still lay sleeping, dreaming
Her housewife's dreams.

He filled the glass-knobbed percolator
With cold water, the basket of fresh coffee
Perched on the center, slender limb,
And the house began to fill
With the scent of what he would sip
From a cup at the table, glad to be alone
Writing a list of what would be a definition to his day.

I never liked coffee, but I loved my father,
And I would get up in a child's nightgown
And stand on a child's stool
To toast some golden bread
That I could dip into his coffee
Without talking. He would scribble
A few notes, and I would dunk and watch—
No other place I would rather be
Than just sitting there *with him*.

Hives

Up inside the steep ceiling
Of my small front porch, the bees
Have begun to build the tiniest hives,
Which my coming and my going
And my opening the door and closing it
Disturbs. Everything is so attached
To something larger in this world—
Everything becomes a part
Of what it is attached to.

Loneliness can settle inside a human life,
And I want to say, *I am huge with loneliness.*
I want to say, *I am the house*
In which loneliness resides. I had a friend
Who said, *I don't get lonely, anymore,*
As if he had achieved a status of inhumanity.
But I walk into my loneliness like an ant
Across a glacier, like a single sail
Plowing an ocean of blue water.

And sometimes I watch in the evening
As the bees fly back into their paper nests,
And the shades drop down over the windows
Of my neighbors, and the warm yellow glow
Of their televisions is like company talking
In those closed homes.

Then, I can't see beyond my yard
Where three old trees grow thicker
Every year, and my life doesn't seem like much
And my own name seems strange to me,
Like a song in a foreign language I sing into the dark.

Makeup Counter

She must be at least in her seventies,
Plump and grandmotherly—
If I could smell her clothing,
She would carry the faint scent
Of vanilla and cinnamon cookies,
A plate of which she took to neighbors.

And the stylish younger woman
Smoothing a tinted foundation
On the older woman's forehead and chin
Works with the careful strokes
Of a painter, moving along the temples
To the jawline, concealing shadow,
Pulling the high cheekbones forward.

I love the courage it must have taken
For an old woman to be publicly transformed,
And I love how she stares squarely into her own face,
As if she has volunteered to enter
The futile pageants of beauty.

The younger woman paints and daubs
And tints, while the other holds perfectly still,
The girl in her wanting not the beauty
Of youth, but the beauty she already possesses
To be shined up, like tarnished silver.
There, says the sales clerk,
Laying down her brushes and handing the mirror
To what seems like an excited bride,
Who in a quivering voice turns to me and asks,
How do you think I look?

Dusk

Just as the halogen light
On the back porch flickers
Like a struck match, then flares
And catches, the sun also sputters
On the rim of the horizon. Though my light
Is artificial, the street lamps, too,
Halo the alley with a spooky orange glow.
Somewhere, there is always light
To cast the world into shadows.

Even in Italy, the dusk
Comes with the same rituals:
A stutter, a glow, then the city
Lit again. Even in Asia,
A woman lights a candle;
In Africa fire heats a kettle.

And the cliché of the drawn moths
Becomes a universal truth.

Yesterday, my son was born—
Years ago—and when I wait in the restaurant
From an entering crowd I see his face,
A light among the strangers
Before he bent from his tall, young height
Like breaking morning.

Sister

She has settled into middle age
Wearing earrings to her shoulders,
Clothing that conceals how her body
Has softened and grown round
With wealth, opinionated but lacking
Knowledge, so the complexities
Of the world are simplified,
Like a child swimming the surface
Of a lake thinking nothing
Lies beneath the mirror on which she floats.

When she doesn't approve of me
Now, she doesn't hit: she only looks
As if I didn't exist, as if I
Were a common fly annoying the fruit
As it ripens in the bowl.
What have I done
That her hatred takes such aim?
I place the bread, the cheese and walnuts
Carefully arranged on a plate
For her lunch, hoping she'll see
I tried to please her. Because she has no child,
No husband, she thinks she has escaped
Being like our mother. *You were born,*
She means to say, *You ruined my life.*

Eden

Warm and still, with nothing stirring,
I can look into my backyard
And see my father standing beneath
The old apple tree, his pruner
Gripped in one gloved hand,
The other shielding his eyes from the sun.

That was the day I made him cry—
A grown man weeping—not because I
Was harsh, but because I asked
Why he had brought me into this world
Knowing, by then, how she hated
The ones who made her a mother.

I wanted you, was how he answered,
And if I could take back that question,
Un-ask it, holding it still within me
Like a good student not speaking
Out of turn, I'd not be weeping today
Because I made him sad when he was happy
To be helping his daughter
In his coveralls and Southern drawl.

Father ghost, come back.
The boughs are touching the roof now
Like fingers reading Braille,
And the hedge is climbing skyward;
All manner of birds are quarreling
And robbing the berries, and I miss you.

Where is your truck with its magic tools
And gadgets, and who am I without you?
You old, Irish Christian, this Eden
Is beautiful, and I won't ask.

Thief

On the top shelf of our hall closet
Where a child would have to stand on a chair
To find what might be hidden there my father kept his candy.
I broke the laws of that house and felt along in the darkness
Until my hand found, and my hand removed,
The wrapped bars, and I ate them in his absence.
Oh, little primitive, devouring the heart of a lion
To feel his courage and his power.

Maybe I missed him those long days when summer
Was fishing in the creek and building forts
In the trees, but I stole the pleasure he withheld,
I righted the wrong of his selfishness.
So, maybe it was a moral act, my taking from the rich
And giving to the little children,
Like Jesus with his loaves and fishes.

Knowing a belt slapping across bare legs
Would be my punishment, because all good things
Are followed by pain, because his job was to teach
That desire must be broken, even the desire to live.

Three Pair of Shoes and Two Hats

The staff tells me he has asked all day to *go home*,
And I find my father in a short hall
Off to the side of the communal room,
Walking slowly, as if he were carrying a baby,
With three pair of shoes and two hats cradled in his arms.

     I say, *Dad, let's sit down and discuss this,*
     And lead him to a chair. He's happy to see me
     For I am news arriving from his life,
     Someone to remind him of who he is
     And who he was. His gray metal toolbox

Waits in my garage, the hammer
For nailing things up, the measuring tape
That snaps back into its silver casing
Could give this hall a measurable distance
So when he walks, we'd know how far.

Salesman

Look at the two Jehovah's Witnesses heading toward your door
With their little black satchels, selling God on a day in early autumn

Where October makes you long for summer and the past.
They might be neuroscientists of the pre-Prozac era

Promising a long life, a good mood, or a way to save your marriage,
But you want to hide behind the curtains and not come out

In the same way the national debt crisis makes you hit the button
On the radio so that the whole room goes silent.

I am sick of information. As the blinds go down on another season
And another year, I stack the lawn chairs inside the garage

And rake the leaves as if sweeping after a party, feeling like a janitor.
I don't need the leaflet hanging on my door about the family-sized

Pepperoni, double-cheese pizza delivered day or night.
Nothing ever does what it says in advertisements; as for being human

There is no cure. But the white banner with bold black letters
Strung across Main Street is billowing in the wind above the traffic

Telling me to donate blood on Wednesday at the local gym,
Though I don't do those things in public. Just give me a recipe for lemon
    bars

So if I follow the instructions and grate the lemon rind carefully
Everything will turn out fine: a perfect crust, firm custard, no promises.

When I Pray

A prayer, like a dream,
Has a person in it,
And when I pray now,
It's for all the people
I couldn't save. A man
I dated, what you would call
A loser, a drunken braggadocio,
A comic—oh how he saddened me.
He was a bad man
With some goodness in him, too,
Because who he was
And who he wanted to be
Were as distant from each other
As a man and his shadow.

Even though I know it's useless,
I do get down on my knees
Sometimes, fold my hands
And lean my forehead into the tips
Of my fingers, compliant,
Submissive to the only power
I dream I know. I ask for change;
I ask for good luck for him,

And maybe I will see him someday
When he has lost his cockiness,
When he is no longer searching
From bed to bed for a little human warmth,
But probably not.

Probably, he will sit
In his recliner and watch the sun go down
On one more day, ash falling from his cigarette
Like all his other losses,

And ice shrinking to a thin blade
In his Scotch, watching *Out of Africa*
And weeping for all the things in life
He didn't get, which are exactly the same
As the things he wasn't willing to give.

My Love of Facts

Of all the facts I love, my favorite
Is that a spider can tune its web, tightening or loosening
The threads, the way you might correct a guitar or a cello.

It all depends on the way the wind blows
Whether a spider reels in the sticky filaments, but they
Are not as helpless as they seem suspended there in the center

Of the radiating wheel of what they've made.
The voyage is difficult in any ship, so the roses that vibrate
In the rain drop their petals, like tiny flags of surrender,

And when my mother was angry she hummed.
When I am afraid I study the textbook of my imagination
In which I find delight in the fact that elephants, we are told,

Mourn their fallen, and the beauty of that sadness
Makes me love the world a little more than if I did not know it.

The Praise and the Blame

Saturday, I decided to go to attend a church on Sunday
Because there is good music and the singing
Of songs is like the rose-hips and flames of autumn
And the clouds do not represent a cold day
Of rain, but the untouchable substance of the spirit

That simply flows. Though I did not believe all the words
Of the hymns and responses, I stood among the very old
And the very young with their respective sorrows and their hopes
To praise sunlight on the leaves in the garden
And to mourn that, even then, it was passing.

Somehow, it all got mixed up with my father
Who allowed so much to happen and all my anger
Toward God felt like my father's anger toward me.
And I thought, as the priest blessed the bread,

What about the story of the woman with the bruised face
And the children with belted welts across their little bodies—
Is there a story about them in this big book?
But, of course, no one would have told that story:
They would have hidden in a tent from the rest of the tribe.

Inoculation

I don't know what brought me here, but the parking lot
Of St. Andrew's is full of Toyotas, so Episcopalians
Must believe in economy over the roominess of a van.

Whatever I was thinking, I was looking for safety
And a little holiness after watching Miley Cyrus twerk;
I had wanted that man to look into my face as we spoke,

But he wasn't really listening, and his eyes followed
My thigh upward, as if running his finger along a map
To the point where my legs meet. I know it isn't fashionable

To speak of the human soul and its love of innocence;
I know all about hook-ups and one-night stands
Where the body is a feast for lonely, single people,

But I stared that man down somewhere between the elliptical machine
And the treadmill—I stared him down until he walked
Away, sulking near the weights where some guy in a spandex girdle

Was grunting under two hundred pounds of lead. I can't believe
I'm kneeling as the priest lays a wafer on my tongue
And tips the silver chalice to release a tiny sip

Of cheap red wine, as if I'm being inoculated against
The daily violations of this world, as if they could be washed away
Or scrubbed like a stain in a tablecloth, as if I could get

That image of him out: Licking his lips, as if he had tasted something
   sweet.

Descent

He lowers himself down
The invisible filament
To land on the vast white landscape
Of the stove, his several legs
Swimming against the heated porcelain
Of the oven he couldn't know
Was there. Then, almost flailing, he
Raises himself the same way he came, like a climber
On the face of a glacier
To a ledge of safety.

Soon, he tries again, descending
From the hood of the fan
Above the burners, a little more
Slowly this time, as if he can't believe
What he is feeling, as if he can think
What he wanted to find there into being.

Each time he touches the burning surface,
He weakens, his panic
Becoming a giving in, a surrender.
Probably, he is an ounce of body
Held by the curling eyelashes
Of his limbs, and I realize he is cooking in air,
And I take the then pencil
Of a chopstick and let his thread
Attach to that and move him
To the coolness of the sink
Where he rests in that silver mercy.

I do not know the life span
Of a spider or an ant;
I do not believe he embodies
The soul of someone's grandmother,

But I can see the cruelty
Of something blindly dying,
And I rush to intervene, *imitatio dei.*

Whoosh

I don't know exactly what brought me out in the middle
Of the night to gaze at the sky from the back steps,

As if I had lost something, as if I needed something truer
Than the dream I was having about a woman with a face

Covered with tattoos, but the clouds were passing over
Pale as a cataract, and in the clear spots stars looked

Down over the land of the living, and I could hear my neighbors
Making love in the private dark. From the cherry tree,

I heard the *whoosh* of wide wings, the air swept with feathers—
As it crossed the yard and disappeared, then swept

Again to roost among the fidgeting leaves. *Whoosh. Whoosh.*
It moved again, oar in deep water, and I stood listening

And mostly unafraid, as it lowered itself like an old man
Into the branches. I waited for it to tell me what it was:

Injured owl, hurt hawk, unholy ghost of my dead father
Come back to tell me of the fate he hadn't known awaited him.

Multitudes

The hippie woman is standing next to a woman in red stilettos
Waiting to cross at the stoplight, and you can almost smell

Patchouli mixed with Prada suspended in a sweet cloud
Above their heads, the Jesus-sandals of the one,

The tightly clutched purse of the other: two women
Making their statements on the main street of a small town.

Being a woman, or a man, means making certain choices:
The look of wanting to get laid on the opposite page of a magazine

Telling you to explore the possibilities of kayaking,
And it confuses me, the daughter of Baptists, raised

Like an immigrant who wants to Americanize, who also wants
To feel the ocean slipping through the oars

Like a hand moving up my thigh. God, I am odd,
Wrestling the tug of what I should be with the urge

To be myself, watering the plants like an earth-mother
Then flirting as if I were vapid. Forget the women on the corner.

I am snipping the roses to sink their long legs into a vase
On the table: cruel of me to separate them from their original thorns.

Karen Whalley is the author of *The Rented Violin* (Ausable Press). She is a graduate of Warren Wilson MFA Program for Writers, and recipient of the Rona Jaffe Award for Poetry. Her poems have appeared in *The Sun Magazine, American Poetry Review, Mississippi Review, Florida Review,* and other journals. She lives in Port Angeles, Washington.